THEY DIED TOO YOUNG

KURT COBAIN

Andrew Gracie

CHELSEA HOUSE PUBLISHERS
Philadelphia

161   7857

First published in traditional hardback edition
© 1998 by Chelsea House Publishers.
Printed in Hong Kong
Copyright © Parragon Book Service Ltd 1995
Unit 13–17, Avonbridge Trading Estate, Atlantic Road
Avonmouth, Bristol, England BS11 9QD

Illustrations courtesy of Rex Features

Library of Congress Cataloging-in-Publication Data
Gracie, Andrew.
    Kurt Cobain / by Gracie Andrew.
      p.   cm. — (They died too young)
    Originally published: Bristol, England : Parragon Books,
    1995.
    Summary: Chronicles the brief career and mysterious
suicide of the pioneer of grunge music.
    ISBN 0-7910-4634-6
    1. Cobain, Kurt, 1967-1994—Juvenile literature. 2. Rock
musicians—United States—Biography—Juvenile literature.
[1. Cobain, Kurt, 1967-1994. 2. Musicians. 3. Rock music.]
I. Title. II. Series.
ML3930.C525G73   1997
782.42166'092--dc21
    [B]   97-20987
                                             CIP
                                        AC MN

CONTENTS

On Tuesday, April 5, 1994, Kurt Cobain blew his head off with a shotgun. The body was discovered on April 8. The police had to use fingerprints to make a positive ID; dental records were no use. As the news spread, the story took on echoes of other violent celebrity deaths. As with the assassination of John F. Kennedy, many people would remember where they were when Kurt Cobain shot himself.

Through his music Kurt had become an icon, a symbol for the young of their politics and aspirations. He could not cope with this elevation to leader of an entire generation. He made this clear in the suicide note found beside his body. "I haven't felt the excitement of listening to music along with really writing something for years now. I feel guilty beyond words about these things. The fact is I can't fool you. It simply isn't fair to you or to me. The worst crime I could think of would be to put people off by faking it, by pretending I am having 100 percent fun. Sometimes I feel as if I should have a punch-in time clock before I walk on stage. I still can't get out the frustration, the guilt, and the empathy I have for everybody. There's good in all of us and I simply love people too much. So much that it makes me feel too . . . sad, a little sensitive, unappreciative."

Having painted this paradox of the rock star who did not want to be a rock star, at the same time he conformed to all rock star expectations. The note finished, "So remember: It's better to burn out than to fade away." With this quotation from "Out of the Blue, Into the Black," Kurt Cobain placed himself directly in the tradition of other rock deaths—Jim Morrison, Jimi Hendrix, or The Sex Pistol's Sid Vicious. The song had been written in 1978 by Neil Young in despair following the death of Elvis Presley and the rise of punk. Ironically it was precisely through the fusion of punk and seventies rock that Kurt Cobain and Nirvana would transform rock music in the nineties.

The irony would not have escaped him. After all, Kurt would often sign into hotels with his wife, Courtney Love, as Mr. and Mrs. Simon Ritchie, Sid Vicious's real name. However, there could be no irony in the heroin addiction that dogged the last two years of his life and his relationship with Courtney. The autopsy found three times the fatal dose of heroin in his blood. On April 7, before she found out her husband was dead, Courtney Love was rushed to hospital after a suspected overdose and arrested for possession of heroin.

Which is it then? A straightforward rock star drug death, or a tragic figure driven to drugs and eventual suicide by the pressure of fame? Neither provides an adequate explanation of the man and his motivation. For this it is necessary to look further back, to where Kurt was born and to what he was trying escape.

Kurt Cobain as a child in Aberdeen

A ROCKY START

Follow the freeway out of Seattle heading south for California, and after fifty miles appears the sign for Route 12, a highway that winds through the mountains past Olympia down to the coast and Aberdeen. There is little to Aberdeen but trailer parks and logging yards. A drive down main street takes in diners, a five-and-dime, a few bars. Soon enough the town peters out, giving way on one side to endless hillsides of pine and spruce and on the other, at the mouth of the Wishkah river, to the Pacific. The highway stops here, a dead-end in a dead-end town.

It was here that Kurt Cobain was born, on February 20, 1967. His father, Donald, had a good job as a mechanic at the local Chevron station, while his mother, Wendy, kept home in the house the Cobains bought in Aberdeen six months after Kurt was born. The neighborhood was not the best and the family was far from rich, but in Kurt's recollection the period stands out as one of happiness and contentment. Don fixed up the house, laying wall-to-wall carpets and putting in wood paneling and a fake fireplace. "White trash posing as middle class" was how Kurt later described it. His mother was devoted to her first-born, a love Kurt remembered: "My mom was always physically affectionate with me. We always kissed good-bye and hugged. Those were pretty blissful times." When he was three a sister, Kimberley, was added to the Cobain family.

In this stable home environment, Kurt's talents blossomed at an early age. Wendy came from a musical family. Her brother Chuck played in a rock 'n' roll band and her sister Mary played country and western guitar and sang in the bars around Aberdeen. Her uncle Delbert had even recorded ballads in California in the fifties under the name of Dale Arden. Mary gave Kurt Beatles and Monkees records and, when he was seven, a bass drum. He used to strap it on and march around the neighborhood singing Beatles songs. He began drum lessons in third grade. "Ever since I can remember, since I was a little kid, I wanted to be Ringo Starr. But I wanted to be John Lennon playing drums." Mary tried to teach him guitar as well but he had no patience.

In fact, Kurt was diagnosed as hyperactive. To counteract this, he was prescribed Ritalin, a form of speed. Unfortunately, this had the effect of keeping him awake until four in the morning. When sedatives were tried instead, he would fall asleep in school. Yet despite this, he was extremely happy as a young child. As Wendy recalls, "He got up every day with such joy that there was another day to be had. He was so enthusiastic. He would come running out of his bedroom so excited that there was another day ahead of him and he couldn't wait to find out what it was going to bring him."

When Kurt was seven, however, his life changed, and his idyllic childhood ended as Don and Wendy's marriage fell apart. Don was barely around; he was generally either at work or coaching the high school wrestling and basketball teams. Wendy became increasingly resentful and they began to quarrel. Soon after Kurt's eighth birthday his parents separated; by the middle of 1975 they were divorced.

The divorce changed Kurt completely. He became withdrawn and moody. For the first year or so he stayed with his mother and sister in the family home in Aberdeen. But he disliked his mother's new boyfriend; Wendy put this down to

They Died Too Young

jealousy, but Kurt considered him "a huge mean wife-beater." Kurt increasingly ran wild and Wendy lost patience and sent him off to live with Don.

After the divorce Don had gotten a job with a logging company and lived in a trailer in Montesano, twenty miles east of Aberdeen. At first the move worked well. Don and Kurt would go off for camping weekends in the forest or on the beach. When Don had to work weekends, Kurt would tag along. He would sit for hours on end in his father's van listening to tapes on the 8-track player. His favorite was the Queen album *Message to the World*. He would play the tape until the battery was dead, so that when his father came back the van had to be jump-started.

In 1978 Don remarried and Kurt found himself with a stepmother, along with a stepbrother and stepsister. He felt betrayed and developed a violent resentment of his stepmother. Kurt began to cut school, and at home he refused to do chores and he picked on his stepbrother. Don's response was to beat him.

Kurt's one refuge was in music. His taste by this stage had gone beyond The Beatles and The Monkees. Don had been persuaded by a workmate to join the Colombia House record club. After the first free offer he soon lost interest, but he continued to pay the club bills. Kurt, on the other hand, was hooked. Each month another package would come in the mail, bringing that month's recommended record, albums by the likes of Aerosmith, Led Zeppelin, Black Sabbath, and Kiss. This music went along with the only recognizable counterculture in town. To wear a Kiss T-shirt and fleece-lined denim jacket through high school was an established way to rebel.

Kurt was also inspired by the new movement from England known as punk. He had never heard any of the music but he would read all he could about it, cutting out articles from *Creem* magazine on Richard Hell, Iggy Pop, and The Sex Pistols. He managed to track down one punk record, the Clash album *Sandanista*. When he got it home, he was bitterly disappointed. This was not what he thought punk should sound like.

For his fourteenth birthday, his uncle Chuck made him an offer: he could either have a bike or a guitar. Kurt took the guitar, a secondhand electric that barely played. He took lessons for a week, long enough to learn how to play AC/DC's "Back in Black." From this he moved on to working out "Louie Louie" and "Another One Bites the Dust." He wrote his own songs too, trying to imagine what punk would really be like: "I tried to play as nasty as I could. Turn my little ten-watt amplifier up as loud as it could go." His punk introduction was not long in coming.

The bands in Aberdeen were basically cover bands, with the exception of The Melvins. Formed around 1981, The Melvins were named after a man named Melvin who was arrested for stealing a Christmas tree from the Montesano Thriftway. Initially they tried to play like the Ramones—three-minute songs at 90 mph without too many chord changes. However, soon the music they were steeped in—Kiss and Black Sabbath—took hold. While the rest of the punk world played super-fast, the Melvins got slower and heavier. As Buzz Osborne, the lead singer, said, "It was so backward, it was forward." But Aberdeen was not ready for punk or the Melvins. Their shows never drew a crowd of more than fifty. All the same, to many kids, Kurt included, they were heroes, the closest thing in Aberdeen to rock stars. Their rehearsals became a regular hangout, a social scene for the town's rebels. Kurt more than most became devoted to the band, going to every gig and helping with their equipment.

For his part, Buzz turned Kurt on to good music, giving him compilation tapes of southern California punk, bands like Flipper and MDC. Kurt was blown away. "It was like listening to something from a different planet. It took me a few days to accept it." In fact, he swallowed it whole. In

They Died Too Young

August 1984 Black Flag played the Mountaineer Club in Seattle. Kurt sold his record collection to get the $12 together for a ticket, driving up to Seattle with The Melvins in their tour van for the gig. When he came back he spiked his hair and decided to form a band.

Kurt's sense of a worthwhile vocation was not shared by his parents. Sick of being passed around from relative to relative, he begged his mother to take him back. In 1984 Wendy had married Pat O'Connor, a longshoreman with a drinking problem. She didn't think she could deal with her new situation as well as with Kurt, but she was eventually persuaded to let him come home. Her apprehension was well founded. Kurt spent his time cutting school, smoking dope, and arguing with her constantly. He would spend hours on end in his bedroom, playing guitar with the amp at full volume. Whenever Wendy returned from work she was met with complaints from the neighbors. Soon she lost patience again and told him to go. He went back to live with Don, who insisted that he give up music and tried to make him join the navy instead. It was no surprise that Kurt lasted in Montesano for a week. After that he did not see his father again for the next eight years. And school was no better: he flunked out in May 1985, six weeks before graduation.

Cobain on stage with Nirvana in the early days

ALL THE INGREDIENTS OF GRUNGE

After flunking out of school he got a job (ironically as a caretaker at Aberdeen High) and with a friend rented an apartment in Aberdeen. But then the job became boring, the friend moved out, and, months behind with the rent, Kurt was evicted. During the winter of 1985 Kurt survived on $40 of food stamps a month, sleeping under the North Aberdeen Bridge. He used the stamps to buy beer and lived off food he could scrounge or fish from the river. He subsequently played down the memory: "I was just living out the Aberdeen fantasy version of being a punk rocker. It was really easy. It was nothing compared to what most kids are subjected to after they run away to the big city. There was no threat of danger, ever."

Part of the fantasy was graffiti. He would drink and then go out at night and paint slogans on the walls around Aberdeen. When the police arrested him—spray can in hand, while he was writing on the side of a bank—they found nothing in his pockets but a guitar pick, a can of beer, and a cassette by a punk band. Kurt was given a $180 fine and a thirty-day suspended sentence.

Another part of the fantasy was drugs. He bought from a dealer who got his stock robbing pharmacies. The dealer supplied Kurt with Percodan, a painkiller derived from opium. Kurt had no idea what they were or that they were addictive but by the summer of 1986 he was taking ten a day and, in his own words, "getting real itchy." After two months the dealer's supply ran out and Kurt had to quit cold turkey. That summer he also took heroin for the first time.

Feeling guilty about her son being homeless, Wendy helped Kurt out with the deposit for a roof over his head, this time a broken-down shack. Kurt lived there with Matt Lukin, The Melvins' bassist. They had no refrigerator and only a toaster oven. Neither made any effort to keep the place clean. To make matters worse, Kurt bought six turtles and put them in a bathtub in the middle of the living room. For irrigation he drilled a hole in the floor. Unfortunately the water did not drain but instead started to seep up, rotting the floorboards. There was a constant stench of stagnant water. Between this and the unpaid rent, Kurt was evicted again.

In the meantime he had started going out with Tracy Marander, whom he had met through Buzz Osborne at a punk club in Seattle. When he was evicted he moved in with Tracy in her small studio apartment in Olympia, Washington. To earn money, Kurt was desperate enough to start a covers band called the Sellouts to play Creedence Clearwater Revival songs in Aberdeen bars. In fact, the band never played. Kurt fell out with the bass player, who later lost his fingers in a logging accident. Undeterred by the loss of their bassist, Kurt and Chris Novoselic (the six-foot-seven half-Croatian with whom Kurt would eventually form Nirvana) persevered, bringing in Aaron Burckhard to play drums. With this lineup, from late 1987 on, they began to make headway. Kurt had written a strong set of songs— "Hairspray Queen," "Spank Thru," "Downer," and "Floyd the Barber" among them—and they began to develop a following. They played under the various names of Skid Row, Throat Oyster, Windowpane, and Bliss. Then they hit on Nirvana.

Kurt and Chris began to believe in what they were doing. Chris and his girlfriend, Shelli, moved into the apartment in

Olympia with Kurt and Tracy so the two band members could practice every night. Kurt even got a job as a caretaker so they could save some money to make a demo. But they had drummer trouble. They could not get Aaron Burckhard out of Aberdeen (he was not happy about driving the forty miles to Olympia every night just to practice) nor Aberdeen out of him (he wanted to play heavy metal and Led Zeppelin covers in particular). His unreliability was worst at the beginning of the month, when his girlfriend's welfare check came in and they would go out and live it up.

When Burckhard was not around, they played when they could with The Melvins' drummer, Dale Crover, but in early 1988 he went off with the rest of The Melvins to live in San Francisco. Before he went he recommended Dave Foster, who turned out to be into heavy metal and fond of a brawl. His time in Nirvana was short-lived, though he only found out he had been dropped when he saw an ad for a Nirvana gig in the local paper. The band had found another drummer, Chad Channing.

Nirvana's sound was not born in a vacuum. While punk left no obvious mark on Seattle, there were some who had been listening and the legacy of grassroots independence and self-expression encouraged them, talented or not, to play. Like everywhere else in the States, college radio became keeper of the flame, playing the canon of English-import punk classics and giving air time to local bands. In an attempt to regain the purity of 1977, punk went hardcore in the mid-eighties. This orthodoxy demanded a pared-back, no frills sound and speed-fueled two-minute songs. Since punk had never really happened in the Pacific Northwest, its adulteration was never really a cause for concern. Instead the ethos was fused with the seventies rock that in Seattle had never really gone away, a style that was christened Grunge.

By January 1988, Kurt and Chris had saved enough to make a demo. They went to Reciprocal Recordings, a broken-down studio at the home of Jack Endino, house producer for Sub Pop records and as such godfather of the Seattle sound. Endino was a punk believer: he did not produce records, he just recorded them and charged next to nothing for the service. This rough-and-ready quality became a defining characteristic of Grunge. With Dale Crover on drums, they laid down and mixed ten songs in six hours. The demo cost only $152 but Kurt was happy with the way it turned out.

Endino really liked the tape too. He made a remix and gave a copy to Jonathan Poneman of Sub Pop. At the time Sub Pop was anxious to sign new bands to fill out their roster, and Poneman was excited by what he heard. Nirvana was fresh and came from outside the insular Seattle scene.

Kurt had not even considered signing with Sub Pop. He wanted to sign with one of the indie labels that his heroes were with: SST in California or Touch & Go in Chicago. He sent off tapes to these companies but got no reply. Then Poneman got in touch, saying he had heard the tape, liked it, and wanted to put out a single. A meeting was arranged at the Café Roma in Seattle. Kurt and Tracy turned up early. Poneman remembers Kurt as being "very timid and respectful," "a very nice gentle guy." Chris arrived late. He had been drinking to calm his nerves, and throughout the meeting he glared at Poneman, breaking in every so often to insult him loudly. Despite Chris's onslaught, a deal was arranged for Sub Pop to put out Nirvana's first record.

The band (by this time Chad Channing was their drummer) went back into the studio with Jack Endino in June 1988. The track selected for the single was "Love Buzz," a cover of a song by Shocking Blue, an obscure Dutch psychedelic band from the sixties. However, Sub Pop was overextended and had serious cashflow problems. Months passed and still the Nirvana single was not released. Kurt would phone Poneman, who would promise again that it would be released soon, until Sub Pop eventually found the money and the record came out in November.

Grunge fashion

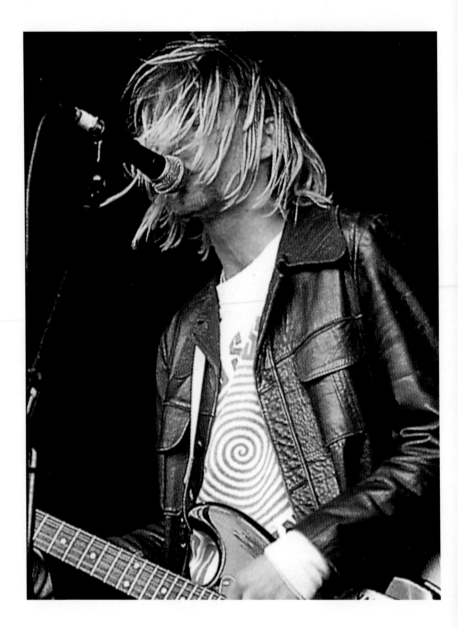

Kurt Cobain on stage

ON AN INCREASING HIGH

Encouraged by the success of the single, Nirvana started rehearsing songs for what was to become their first album, *Bleach*. Sub Pop said they had no money. Despite this, Kurt went ahead and booked a studio with Endino. They started recording on Christmas Eve and by early January had finished the ten tracks. Since Kurt had not finished writing the lyrics when they went into the studio, several of the songs consisted of no more than one verse repeated two or three times. Kurt put this down to expediency. He also claimed that there was nothing personal about the songs. Despite this, many reflect his Aberdeen upbringing.

In "Swap Meet" Kurt sings about a sight common in parking lots in small-town America: people selling what they can secondhand to raise a buck. Kurt described them as people "who can't look further than selling junk because they live in junk. They're surrounded by it and their whole mentality is based on junk—grease, dirt and poverty." In other songs he lashed out at his current concerns. "School" was aimed at the Seattle scene, where it meant social death not to listen to the right bands, to hold the right views, and be seen with the right people. The chorus "You're in high school again" is repeated over and over. There was an added irony in making the record sound as much like Grunge was supposed to sound as they could. "We wrote it about Sub Pop. If we could have thrown in Soundgarden's name, we would have," Kurt said later, complaining that they had written songs to fit in with what Sub Pop expected of them. At the same time, flashes of Nirvana's future direction came through. "About the Girl" in particular is unashamedly melodic. Tracy had asked Kurt why he didn't write a song about her; this was his response.

The album cost $606 to record. Afterward Nirvana was due to go on a two-week tour around the Northwest, including a gig in San Francisco. At the time, the city authorities were running a big anti-AIDS campaign encouraging heroin users to "bleach their works." This provided them with the name for the album. Sub Pop released *Bleach* in June 1989. Initial reaction to the album was muted but gradually sales picked up.

For their first U.S. tour, they all piled in a white van and took turns with the driving. They had no road crew, no one to sort out where they were going to eat or sleep. They played tiny venues and often hardly anyone turned up. But to Kurt the whole thing was an adventure: "We were totally poor but, God, we were seeing the United States for the first time. And we were in a band and we were making enough money to survive. It was awesome." Their poverty was not helped by their penchant for smashing equipment, but this quickly became a Nirvana ritual and a standard part of the set.

Later in the year they made their first trip to Europe, touring with another Sub Pop band, TAD. Starting in Newcastle, England, they played thirty-six shows in forty-two days. Most of the time was spent crammed in a Fiat van driving between gigs. Although they played to big crowds, the shows were a strain. They had to put up with poor equipment, the result of their vicious cycle of smashing their instruments, which then had to be repaired or replaced for the next night. Kurt spent most of the tour drunk or asleep. By the time they reached Rome, Kurt was ready to snap, ground down by the tight schedule, the poor food, the cramped bus, and the poor equipment. Four songs into the set he smashed his guitar, walked off stage, and climbed a speaker stack. He

They Died Too Young

threatened to jump before setting off hand over hand across the rafters, screaming at the audience below. He finally reached a balcony, from where he was eventually persuaded to come backstage. The band was allowed a few days off after that before completing the tour in London.

As well as playing on his nerves, Kurt's long absences on tour had put a strain on his relationship with Tracy. Halfway through the second U.S. tour in April 1990 Kurt called Tracy from Amherst, Massachusetts, to tell her he was moving out. When the tour ended, Kurt started to go out with Tobi Vail. Although a couple of years younger than Kurt, Tobi was an impressive figure. She helped start the Riot Grrl movement, which through music and fanzines tried to promote feminism in rock (the sexist rock press soon dubbed it Foxcore) and had a definite influence on Kurt's own political thinking. However, the relationship did not last and they split up in November 1990. Kurt, though only twenty-three at the time, wanted more commitment.

Kurt had been writing songs toward a second album, moving beyond the formulaic Grunge of *Bleach* to find a blend of a heavy sound with melody. In April 1990 they made a first recording of the new material with Butch Vig at his studio in Wisconsin. The session revealed the shortcomings in Chad's drumming. He could not deliver the big drum sound that Kurt and Chris wanted and sometimes could not play the parts that were written for him. When they came back to Seattle Chad was fired and Nirvana was on the lookout for a drummer again. Soon after this the hardcore band Scream broke up. Kurt and Chris had once seen Scream play and had been impressed by drummer David Grohl. They invited him up to Seattle to audition. The moment they began to play together Kurt and Chris realized that the final piece of the Nirvana sound was in place.

As bootleg copies of the sessions recorded with Butch Vig made the rounds, Nirvana was hotly pursued by the major record labels. They were wined and dined, flown to New

Kurt Cobain was a big fan of Sonic Youth

York and Los Angeles. Having decided to part company with Sub Pop, the band was delighted with the attention. To negotiate the best possible deal, they first signed with a management agency, Gold Mountain, who also handled Sonic Youth, long-standing heroes of Kurt's who had become friends of the band. They had come to see the New York show in Nirvana's first U.S. tour in 1989 and in August 1990 asked the band to support them on a short West Coast tour. It was thus no surprise that they should influence Nirvana in persuading them to sign for their label, Geffen. Most of the advance of $287,000 went to taxes, legal fees, and meeting debts. At the same time Geffen paid $75,000 to Sub Pop to buy the band out of its contract with them.

The deal with Geffen was not signed until April 1991. Through the winter the band stayed in Seattle, surviving on the $1000 a month doled out by Geffen ahead of their advance. Kurt and Dave shared the apartment in Olympia, leaving it only to practice with Chris on material for the new album. Kurt had black memories of the period. "The whole winter that Dave and I spent together in that little apartment was the most depressing time I'd had in years. It was so . . . small and dirty and cold and gray . . . I just couldn't handle it. I was so bored and poor. We were signed to Geffen for months and we didn't have any money. We ended up having to pawn our amps and our TV, all kinds of stuff, just to get money to eat corn dogs. It just felt really weird to be signed to this multimillion-dollar corporation and be totally poor. All we did was practice. It was the only thing that saved us. Even that got repetitious after awhile."

The other consolation Kurt turned to was heroin. Because he spent most of his time asleep during that period, it took a while for anyone to notice. But once on a visit to the Olympia apartment Tracy found him passed out on the bathroom floor, his sleeve rolled up and a spoon in the sink. Chris and Dave made it clear that they did not approve of his drug taking. Kurt did not stop; he just tried to hide his habit.

Nirvana in concert

THE TEEN SPIRIT TAKES OFF

In April 1991 the band went down to Los Angeles to record the new album with Butch Vig. The change of climate and the chance at last to go to work on the new record brought a change in mood. Besides, Kurt did not know any dealers in L.A. so he was off the heroin. The drum and bass parts were laid down in the first few days of recording; Kurt was kept longer doing vocals and guitar overdubs and writing lyrics. Much of the material came from their session the year before with Vig. The arrangements were largely unchanged, though many of the lyrics were rewritten. Kurt as usual was self-deprecating about the creative process, saying that mostly they "just lounged on the couch in the recreation area of the studio for days on end just writing lyrics here and there."

Out of this process was born "Smells Like Teen Spirit." The song was started from a riff that Kurt hit upon in the studio; the drum and bass parts were built around it. At first it struck them as nothing remarkable. If anything they feared there would be accusations of ripping off The Pixies in having quiet verses juxtaposed with loud, manic choruses. However, when the band heard the playback they knew they were on to something. The song opens with a staccato guitar riff, swamped by the entry of drums, bass, and distorted guitar. A murmured verse follows, tailing off in a sneering "Hello, Hello, Hello. . . ." Then suddenly the chorus erupts with Kurt screaming almost unintelligibly, "With the lights out, it's less dangerous/Here we are, now entertain us/I feel stupid and contagious/Here we are, now entertain us/A mulatto, an albino, a mosquito, my libido." On the page the lyrics make little sense, but set against the raw emotion of the music the whole somehow comes together. As Kurt saw it, the song was about his audience and the band in relation to that audience. With the title "Smells Like Teen Spirit" and the opening line "Load up on guns and bring your friends," it is a song of revolution, a call to arms. On the other hand, Kurt was reacting to the pressure on him to be some sort of political spokesman; he sings, "I found it hard, it was hard to find/Oh well whatever never mind " and ends up repeating over and over "a denial, a denial." In other words, it may smell like teen spirit but it is not the real thing. The fact that Teen Spirit is a brand of deodorant adds to this sarcasm.

Kurt again addressed the ambivalent relationship he had with his audience on the next track, "In Bloom." The chorus hits out at the rock fans that the band was beginning to attract who had little sympathy with Kurt's punk roots: "He's the one who likes all the pretty songs/And he likes to sing along/And he likes to shoot his gun/But he knows not what it means." The irony is that the tune is so good that it is hard not to sing along. The rest of the album reaches similar heights, and the range and intensity of Kurt's writing demonstrates how much his style had developed since *Bleach*.

When *Nevermind* was finished, everyone was pleased with the result. They knew it was good; though they wouldn't find out until "Smells Like Teen Spirit" was released in September exactly how good. As a result the summer of 1991 found them optimistic and full of confidence. They toured Europe supporting Sonic Youth, playing England's Reading Festival. Kurt summed it up: "The most exciting time for a band is right before they become really popular. I'd love to be in bands that just do that every two years. Every time I look back at the best times in this band it was right before *Nevermind* came out. It was awesome."

They Died Too Young

Kurt had another reason for feeling good. He had started seeing Courtney Love. They had in fact met two years before at a gig in Portland, Oregon. Nirvana was playing support for another band. Courtney recalled Kurt as "hot in a Sub Pop rock god sort of way" while Kurt remembered "She looked like Nancy Spungen . . . a classic punk rock chick." The comparison had not escaped others. Nancy Spungen was the girlfriend of Sid Vicious. Already a well-known punk groupie, she became the first lady of punk and their stormy relationship was followed with all the attention of a royal marriage. She introduced him to heroin and their lives took a downward spiral that ended when Spungen was found stabbed to death in their suite at the Chelsea Hotel in New York. After two months on Rykers Island, charged with her murder, Sid Vicious overdosed while out on bail.

Courtney had an almost mythical past. Daughter of Grateful Dead roadie Hank Harrison, at the age of three she appeared on the back of the Dead's *Aoxomoxoa* album. Later, after her parents split up, her mother took her from L.A. to New Zealand, to Australia, and then back to the States, where Courtney wound up in an Oregon reform school. During her teens she supported herself as a stripper, traveling from Portland to Japan and Ireland. By 1981 she was in Liverpool, hanging out with Echo and the Bunnymen and Julian Cope. She then moved back to the States, where she sang in a succession of bands in between landing parts as a movie actress, in *Sid and Nancy* and then *Straight to Hell,* which featured The Pogues, Joe Strummer, and Elvis Costello. In 1990 she founded her own band, Hole.

There was no doubt from the first meeting that the two were attracted. She was friends with Dave Grohl and confessed to him her feelings for Kurt. Through him she sent Kurt a heart-shaped box filled with seashells, pinecones, and miniature teacups. They met again in May 1991 at a Butthole Surfers gig. As a greeting Courtney punched Kurt in the stomach. He punched her back, then he leaped on her and they began to wrestle. According to Courtney, "It was a mating ritual for dysfunctional people." During the recording of *Nevermind* she dropped by the recording studio a few times. Afterward, when he was away on tour in Europe, she would call him, though at the time she was going out with Billy Corgan, lead singer of The Smashing Pumpkins.

Nevermind was released, with "Smells Like Teen Spirit" as the first single, in September 1991. No one was prepared for the impact it would have. On alternative-music stations, the song quickly became an anthem. WOZQ, the college station in New England, once played the record sixty-seven times in a single week (including once on a reggae show). More important, MTV picked up on the video. It appeared first in their "Buzz Bin," but the audience reaction was so positive that soon they played the video five or six times a day. *Nevermind* opened at 144 on the *Billboard* chart; by December it had reached number one, selling over 300,000 copies a week. *Alternative Press* best captured the mood: "In September 1991 Nirvana were just a local cult, the latest alternative morsel to drop down Geffen's gullet. By October they were U2 and Springsteen, Presley and the Pistols rolled into one snarling bundle."

Cobain unplugged

Courtney Love on stage with Hole

LOVE AND DESTRUCTION

Their lives were transformed. That autumn, touring the States to promote the album, they found their audience increasingly made up of heavy metal kids and Guns N' Roses fans. The change did not agree with Kurt. "I found myself being overly obnoxious during the *Nevermind* tour because I noticed that there were more average people coming into our shows and I didn't want them there. They started to get on my nerves." To compensate they stepped up the guitar-smashing. "We were feeling so weird because we were being treated like kings so we had to destroy everything."

After the U.S. tour they went back to Europe. Kurt was disillusioned and was soon bored with touring. So he turned to Courtney—Hole was on tour in Europe at the same time—and they renewed their telephone romance. Courtney skipped a Hole show just so she could visit Kurt in Amsterdam. Kurt too began to slip up on his band schedule. In Amsterdam Kurt and Courtney turned to heroin. Kurt insisted that it was his idea. In December, when the Nirvana tour ended, Kurt went back to Seattle. Courtney was still in Europe with Hole. Kurt began to do heroin daily, claiming he needed the drug to ease the pain in his stomach, a chronic condition that successive doctors were unable to diagnose or treat. When Courtney flew back from London, he went down to L.A. to be with her.

Frances Bean was born on August 18, 1992

When Nirvana went off on a short tour supporting The Chili Peppers, just after Christmas, Dave and Chris noticed that something was wrong. It was not lost on the press either. The January edition of *BAM* magazine noted that Kurt was "nodding off in mid-sentence," adding that "the pinned pupils, sunken cheeks and scabbed sallow skin suggest something more serious than fatigue." It was in this state that Kurt went to New York to appear on *Saturday Night Live.* His drug use was putting a strain on the band. His moods were erratic, his behavior unreliable. Chris and Dave saw less and less of Kurt, though the band was meant to be going on a tour of Australia and New Zealand at the end of the month.

More importantly, it was at this time that Courtney discovered she was pregnant. She claims that she immediately stopped taking heroin and went to a specialist for a full medical checkup to ensure the baby would be all right. Kurt, too, tried to clean up, going into a detoxification center. But once on tour he experienced stomach problems again and was prescribed physeptone, a kind of methadone.

The tour ended in Hawaii. Kurt and Courtney had decided the time was right to be married. The ceremony took place on a cliff above a beach on February 24, 1992. Kurt had run out of physeptone and had to persuade a friend to bring him some heroin as a wedding present. There were only a handful of people there, including Dave but not Chris. Chris's wife, Shelli, had been more outspoken in blaming Courtney for what had happened to Kurt. Kurt refused to invite her to the wedding, so Chris decided that if his wife was not invited he would not go either.

This estrangement increased after the tour and Chris and Kurt did not talk for about five months. While Chris and Dave went back to Seattle, Kurt and Courtney moved into an apartment in L.A., where Kurt began his daily round of shooting up again. He worked his way up to a $400-a-day habit, the maximum his cash machine would give him. The group came close to splitting up not only because of the drugs but because Kurt demanded a redistribution of the royalties from *Nevermind*. To that point they had been split evenly but Kurt insisted that as songwriter he should be given the lion's share. He demanded 75 percent of all royalties retroactively. Chris and Dave eventually gave in but for a long time afterward the bitterness remained.

From the beginning of the year the press had begun to scent a possible story in Kurt and Courtney as drug addicts. In June Nirvana had to go back to Europe to play some gigs they had skipped the autumn before. The day after the Belfast show, Kurt collapsed and had to be rushed to a hospital. The rumor went around that he had overdosed, though the record label insisted that it was exhaustion. In fact Kurt had forgotten to take his methadone the night before. Despite the fact that he had been on heroin continuously for the preceding six months, questions about drug abuse were still met with flat denials.

All this was in vain, however, when the September edition of *Vanity Fair* hit the newsstands carrying an interview with Courtney by Lynn Hirschberg. Hirschberg portrayed Courtney as a "a charismatic opportunist and proud of it," with a "train-wreck personality." Buried in the later paragraphs of the piece were details of her drug binge with Kurt in New York and the apparent admission that she had taken heroin when she knew she was pregnant. Immediately they were besieged by the press and took refuge by checking into the hospital. Courtney was close to her due date in any case and Kurt wanted to make an attempt to go clean. Gold Mountain tried to minimize the damage, claiming that the pair had only had a brief experimentation with heroin. The world was convinced that they were junkies and that Courtney's baby would be deformed, but on August 18 Frances Bean was born healthy and completely normal. However, following the *Vanity Fair* piece the L.A. County Department of Child Services moved in. Kurt and Courtney were forced to surrender custody of Frances Bean to

They Died Too Young

Courtney's sister. For a month afterward they were not allowed to be alone with their daughter.

It was no surprise that their relations with the press were hostile after this episode, and Kurt gave an effective reply on stage when, a week after Frances's birth, Nirvana headlined at the Reading Festival. Kurt came on in a wheelchair and wearing a hospital gown, sending up press reports regarding his health. Two weeks later they were scheduled to appear at the MTV Music Awards. Kurt wanted to play a new song, "Rape Me," and it was no surprise that MTV refused. It looked as if Nirvana would not appear despite the fact that *Nevermind* was expected to win in a number of categories. At the last minute Kurt relented and agreed to play "Lithium." The appearance went a long way toward dispelling rumors about his addiction. By the end of the year they had managed to persuade the authorities that Frances should be allowed to live with them, though they had to go through the indignity of regular urine tests.

Meanwhile Kurt was preparing songs for a new album. It was now eighteen months since they had finished recording *Nevermind* and the time was right for another album. By this stage Grunge had become mainstream. The charts were dominated by the Seattle sound, with bands like Soundgarden, Alice in Chains, and Pearl Jam. In the process Grunge had lost its edge and its threat to the establishment. It had even taken to the fashion runways, as the December issue of *Vogue* filled its pages with Grunge fashion. This dismayed Kurt. He was determined to make a record that would challenge the audience gathered from *Nevermind*. To this end Steve Albini was chosen as producer. It seemed a strange choice given that Albini was known to hold the opinion that Nirvana was unremarkable, "R.E.M. with a fuzzbox" as he put it. To Kurt, however, he was a legend. Not only had he produced for one of Kurt's favorite bands, The Pixies, but he had played with Big Black, a hugely influential Chicago punk group of the early eighties.

In February 1993 they went to Albini's studio in Minnesota, where they recorded everything within about six days. Most tracks were recorded live with only the minimum of retakes or changes. When the result was handed over to the management at Geffen, they hated it. Kurt was unapologetic, but when he returned from Minnesota he began to have doubts. The bass sound was muddy and the whole seemed to lack finish. It was agreed that some of the tracks should be remixed. Meanwhile Albini gave an interview to the *Chicago Tribune* alleging that Geffen would not release the record. This theme was taken up by *Newsweek,* which reported the rumor that the record was unreleasable. In May, in Seattle, Kurt worked on the remixes with Scott Litt, the producer of R.E.M. In the end only two tracks—"Heart-shaped Box" and "All Apologies"—were significantly changed.

TAKING THE BLAME

When *In Utero* was finally released in September, it may have come as a surprise how listenable the album was, despite the harder edge to the sound. But this could not hide the bitterness and rage in the lyrics, as Kurt took his chance to have his say on the events since *Nevermind*. From the start Kurt laid out his scorn for his fans: "Teenage angst has paid off well/Now I'm bored and old"; for the record company and rock press: "Self-appointed judges judge/More than they have sold"; for critics of Courtney: "If she floats then she is not/A witch like we had thought"; and for the way he and his music were reduced to the product of a broken home: "Serve the servants—oh no/That legendary divorce is such a bore." Where the songs are not enraged, Kurt exhibits a weary acceptance, in particular on "All Apologies," which ends the album with Kurt sounding tired and defeated: "What else should I be/All apologies," and "Everything is my fault/I'll take all the blame."

While the record did not create the same hysterical reaction that had followed the release of *Nevermind*, in a way it did not need to. The members of Nirvana were now thoroughly established MTV darlings and the perceived standard-bearers of the indie scene. There were no surprises: the interviews, reviews, and videos went ahead as they might have done for Guns N' Roses or The Rolling Stones; their tour to promote the album sold out everywhere before they played a note. Kurt could not escape; he had become the kind of rock star he could not stand.

His music still provided a way out to break the boredom. In July 1993 at the New Music Seminar in New York he played an acoustic set. The audience was dismayed, booing and shouting out at him to play some rock music. He followed this in October by appearing in the MTV "Unplugged" series. Again the audience were puzzled: there was no "Smells Like Teen Spirit" but instead covers of old Vaselines numbers and David Bowie's "The Man Who Sold the World." There was a sense of huge potential, that he could turn his hand to anything. Instead what his audience wanted and what the Geffen company was intent to give them was Nirvana.

All that October and November they toured the States. The band was playing well, having added a second guitarist, Pat Smear, to the lineup. Kurt too was in good form, off heroin since May. However, the tour involved long periods of separation from Courtney and Frances Bean and he was frequently remote and abstracted. After Christmas the tour moved to Europe. According to Kurt's wishes, Nirvana was supported in London by the legendary punk band The Raincoats and in France by The Buzzcocks. All went well until the end of February, but then Kurt just seemed to come to a halt. He played badly in Milan and again in Germany. Finally after a concert on March 1 in Munich, he declared he had had enough and would not play again.

He flew down to Rome and checked into the Excelsior Hotel, where Courtney and Frances flew in from London to meet him. But this was not enough to lift his mood. It is not clear what happened, whether they quarreled or about what, but on March 3 Kurt made his first suicide attempt, washing down fifty Rohypnol pills with champagne. Courtney came back the next morning to find him in a coma, a suicide note by his body. Kurt was rushed to the hospital, where after a

Kurt Cobain was found dead at his home outside Seattle

couple of days he made a full recovery. Gold Mountain passed the overdose off as accidental overindulgence; Courtney put it down to a quarrel: "If he thinks he can get away from me like that he can forget it. I'll follow him through hell." Kurt said nothing.

The couple returned to Seattle on March 10. On the surface everything was fine. According to the record company, when Kurt had recuperated Nirvana would play the dates that had been canceled at the end of the European tour. In fact, Kurt was hurtling toward self-destruction at an accelerating pace. Straightaway he was sighted again in his old heroin haunts. Courtney feared that if his drug problem were made public they would lose Frances again. She organized an intervention, gathering friends and family to confront him with his problem and their disapproval. Threatened with divorce by Courtney, he joined her in a twelve-step rehabilitation program in a hospital in Marina Del Rey, California. He lasted three days before he discharged himself, without saying anything to Courtney, and went back to Seattle. He bought a shotgun, claiming he needed it for self-defense, and then disappeared.

Courtney had no idea where he was. For three days she looked for him in L.A. and hired private detectives to search Seattle. As time passed she grew desperate. She called all his friends and his mother, who in turn reported him missing to the Seattle Police. It was too late.

On April 5 Kurt returned to his mansion in Lake Washington Boulevard. He shot up with heroin and valium, then put the shotgun in his mouth and squeezed the trigger with his toe. He was twenty-seven.

It is easy to say that Kurt Cobain died too young. What is harder to see is how he would have lived any longer and kept his sense of integrity. Being the product of a punk tradition had a high price. He wanted to be an outcast, an irritant, to be heard and understood by only a small community of believers that shared his punk ideals. Instead Nirvana had

Fan's gather after Cobain's death

become a bloated rock event as bankrupt, as he saw it, as any of the bands he had come to destroy. Nirvana's arrival in 1991 may have answered a need for a return to something raw and vital, but Nirvana's staying saw them reduced to a convenient symbol for the slacker generation, a template for major labels, and a circus for the media. He loathed himself and despised those around him. In his songs he had taunted his audience from the beginning, and despite his scorn they kept listening. In his rock star death of drugs and suicide he taunted them again: there would be nothing more to listen to.

Seattle, Washington, heart of the Grunge scene

INDEX

INDEX

Alice in Chains, another Seattle band